Dr. Henry W. Williams
Pam 73 Rid with Mr. Waterston's
best regards

I0750944

REMARKS

UPON

THE LIFE AND WRITINGS

OF

CHARLES SPRAGUE.

BY

R. C. WATERSTON.

BEFORE THE
MASSACHUSETTS HISTORICAL SOCIETY,
FEBRUARY 11, 1875.

BOSTON:
PRESS OF JOHN WILSON AND SON.
1875.

REMARKS

UPON

THE LIFE AND WRITINGS

OF

CHARLES SPRAGUE.

BY

R. C. WATERSTON.

BEFORE THE

MASSACHUSETTS HISTORICAL SOCIETY,

FEBRUARY 11, 1875.

BOSTON:
PRESS OF JOHN WILSON AND SON.
1875.

TRIBUTE TO CHARLES SPRAGUE.

Charles Sprague, born Oct. 26, 1791, was eighty-four years of age when he peacefully passed away. The whole of that long life was lived in this community. Year after year went by in a manner which, to many persons, would have seemed monotonous; but each successive day found him engaged in his various duties, with large responsibilities resting upon him; and, when released from these cares, he welcomed most heartily the quiet of home, and asked for no greater privilege than to participate in the affections of his kindred, and to enjoy that intellectual communion which he ever found in books.

His father, Samuel Sprague, was a mechanic, intelligent, laborious, and patriotic, of the same type with Paul Revere and others of that day, — a class of men universally honored for their integrity, sound sense, and public spirit. As a lad he helped throw the British tea into the harbor; as a man he shouldered his musket and fought for the liberties of his country; and, in an after day, with the same skilful hands he helped build the State House, in which our legislative bodies still meet.

His son Charles, until his thirteenth year, attended our public schools, having been a student at the Franklin School, at that time in Nassau Street, on the site now occupied by the Brimmer School. His teachers were Dr. Bullard and Mr. Lemuel Shaw, since so widely known as Chief Justice of the Massachusetts Supreme Court. The opportunities thus granted were the utmost he enjoyed, save that which life and books, and an earnestly energetic and inquiring mind, brought within his reach. At the age of thirteen he left school, and was apprenticed to Messrs. Thayer & Hunt, of whom he gained his first practical knowledge of business. He would at times pleasantly narrate, what was unique in the history of the school, that, on his taking final leave of the school, the teacher gave him his hand, and, turning to the scholars, said, "Charlie has been a good boy, and you may offer him some mark of your kind approbation." Whereupon all the boys loudly applauded, and continued their applause as he walked from the school-room and until he was beyond hearing.

While he was yet a very young man he was one of the singers in the choir of the Old South Church; and, as an indication of the primitive character of the times, he would relate how on special occasions the singers walked in procession through the streets, singing as they walked, while one, who played upon the bass-viol, carried the instrument strapped to his leg, which, after his own fashion, he would play upon, as he went limping along.

Among the singers of the choir was a young lady, Miss Elizabeth Rand, to whom Charles Sprague was engaged, and who in May, 1814, became his wife. [Mr. Waterston here called attention to a volume in manuscript containing some forty pieces of sacred music, both the musical notes, and the words, written out by Mr. Sprague's own hand, — a beautiful and perfect specimen of penmanship. This precious gift was treasured by the lady for life, and it is now equally prized by her children.]

Mr. Sprague was in business for several years in the old Scollay Buildings, near the head of Brattle Street. The lines among his poems entitled "Montague" were addressed to his partner in business. The name is wholly fictitious. In 1820 he became associated with the Suffolk Bank; and when the Globe Bank was established, in 1825, he became an officer in that institution, — a connection which continued unbroken through all the active years of his life.

Such were the external surroundings out of which the intellectual acquirements and the widely extended reputation of Mr. Sprague developed themselves. His earliest literary achievement was the gaining, at six different times, prizes which had been offered for the best poems to be recited on public occasions. Among these was the famous "Shakspeare Ode," delivered in 1823, at the exhibition of a pageant in honor of Shakspeare. The lines are full of graphic power and all aglow with the fire of genius.

This ode was written fifty-two years ago, when Mr. Sprague was thirty-two years of age. [Mr. Waterston placed before the Society the original manuscript, written by the author at that time. It was signed "Airy Nothing," under which signature it gained the prize.] In this manuscript are various alterations by the author's hand, among the most important and curious of which are the closing lines: —

> "Once more in thee shall Albion's sceptre wave;
> And what her mighty Lion lost, her mightier Swan shall save."

Beneath the last line is written in pencil, —

> "*And what her* MONARCH *lost, her* MONARCH BARD *shall save.*"

Mr. Sprague has written upon the manuscript, under date of November 26, 1823, a statement that, if considered too long for recital, there are one or two passages which may be omitted. These he encloses in brackets, marked 1 and 2. This magnificent production at once established the literary reputation of the author. Mr. Sprague also inserted upon the manuscript, "The above was written with some reference to its POSSIBLE publication." It is interesting to read such a sentence now, when, after half a century, these lines have become familiar wherever American literature is known.

The earliest poem of considerable length was delivered forty-six years ago, before the Phi Beta Kappa Society of Cambridge, Aug. 27, 1829, when the author was thirty-eight years of age. This was received with an outburst of enthusiasm at the time, and upon its publication at once took its place as an acknowledged work of pre-eminent merit, while for nearly half a century it has continued to sustain the high place that was at first awarded it. It was remarkable that one who had written for the public so seldom, and whose time was almost wholly engrossed in active business-pursuits, should have been able to produce so ripe and scholarly and thoroughly artistic a work. Not a hasty combination of rhymes to answer a temporary occasion, but a felicitous poem, complete in all its parts, compact with thought, brilliant with wit, weighty with wisdom, graphic in its portrayals, tender in its pathos, and genuine in its humor.

It is worthy to hold companionship with Campbell's "Pleasure of Hope," or Rogers's "Pleasures of Memory." "CURIOSITY" was, in itself, a subject happily chosen; and it was in every respect as happily carried out.

What can be more beautiful than the portrayal of its earliest development in childhood? —

> "In the pleased infant see its power expand,
> When first the coral fills his little hand;

Throned in his mother's lap, it dries each tear,
As her sweet legend falls upon his ear;
Next it assails him in his top's strange hum,
Breathes in his whistle, echoes in his drum;
Each gilded toy, that doting love bestows,
He longs to break and every spring expose.
Placed by your hearth, with what delight he pores
O'er the bright pages of his pictured stores!
How oft he steals upon your graver task,
Of this to tell you, and of that to ask!
And when the warning hour to-bedward bids,
Though gentle sleep sits waiting on his lids,
How winningly he pleads to gain you o'er,
That he may read one little story more!"

The poem is filled with touches of nature like the following: —

"The blooming daughter throws her needle by,
And reads her school-mate's marriage with a sigh;
While the grave mother puts her glasses on,
And gives a tear to some old crony gone."

With how keen a pencil does he sketch the walks of traffic, —

"Where Mammon's votaries bend, of each degree,
The hard-eyed lender, and the pale lendee;
Where rogues insolvent strut in whitewashed pride,
And shove the dupes who trusted them aside."

With what a gracious smile he watches the credulity of the antiquarian who —

"The crusted medal rubs, with painful care
To spell the legend out — *that is not there!*"

The scribe is alluded to at a time when steel pens were not so common as they are now, writing with —

"A quill so noisy and so vain,
We almost hear the goose it clothed complain."

Some of the happy results which have followed the invention of printing are thus briefly hinted: —

"Turn to the Press; its teeming sheets survey,
Big with the wonders of each passing day, —
Births, deaths, and weddings, forgeries, fires, and wrecks,
Harangues and hail-storms, brawls and broken necks;
Where half-fledged bards on feeble pinions seek
An immortality of near a week."

How perfect the picture of the invalid! —

"Behold the sick man in his easy-chair;
Barred from the busy crowd and bracing air,
How every passing trifle proves its power
To while away the long, dull, lazy hour!
As down the pane the rival rain-drops chase,
Curious, he'll watch to see which wins the race;
And let two dogs beneath his windows fight,
He'll shut his Bible to enjoy the sight."

The following solemn description is doubly impressive from the fact that Mr. Sprague had recently lost a beloved brother, who was buried at sea: —

"Wrapped in the raiment that it long must wear,
His body to the deck they slowly bear.
Even there the spirit that I sing is true;
The crew look on with sad, but curious view;
The setting sun flings round his farewell rays,
O'er the broad ocean not a ripple plays;
How eloquent, how awful in its power,
The silent lecture of death's Sabbath-hour!
One voice that silence breaks, — the prayer is said,
And the last rite man pays to man is paid;
The plashing waters mark his resting-place,
And fold him round in one long, cold embrace;
Bright bubbles for a moment sparkle o'er,
Then break, to be, like him, beheld no more."

[Mr. Waterston laid before the meeting the autograph manuscript from which the author read the poem at Cambridge, in 1829, with Mr. Sprague's alterations here and there, showing the severe scrutiny to which he had himself subjected it.]

The next public production was in September, 1830, — forty-five years ago, — when Mr. Sprague was thirty-nine years of age. This was "The Centennial Ode," pronounced at the request of the city authorities before the inhabitants of Boston, at the second centennial from the settlement of the city, at which time Josiah Quincy, then President of Harvard University, delivered the oration.

[The original manuscript from which Mr. Sprague read on that day to the assembled multitude in the Old South Church was here produced, and was examined with evident interest by the members of the Society, not a few of whom remembered the day itself, and listened while the poem was publicly read by the author.] What heart does not throb before his picture of the Pilgrim Fathers? —

"In grateful adoration now,
Upon the barren sands they bow.
What tongue of joy ere woke such prayer
As burst in desolation there?
What arm of strength ere wrought such power
As waits to crown that feeble hour?
There into life an infant empire springs!
There falls the iron from the soul;
There liberty's young accents roll
Up to the King of kings!

Oh! many a time it hath been told,
The story of those men of old,
For this fair Poetry hath wreathed
Her sweetest, purest flower;
For this proud Eloquence hath breathed
His strain of loftiest power;

Devotion, too, hath lingered round
Each spot of consecrated ground,
And hill and valley blessed;
There, where our banished Fathers strayed,
There, where they loved, and wept, and prayed,
There, where their ashes rest.

And never may they rest unsung,
While liberty can find a tongue!
Twine, Gratitude, a wreath for them
More deathless than the diadem,
Who to life's noblest end,
Gave up life's noblest powers,
And bade the legacy descend
Down, down to us and ours."

The lines so widely known and admired under the title of the "Winged Worshippers" were actually written on the fly-leaf of a hymn-book in the old Chauncy-place Church, the Rev. Dr. Frothingham's, where two birds flew through an open window into the church during divine service.

"Gay, guiltless pair,
What seek ye from the fields of heaven?
Ye have no need of prayer,
Ye have no sins to be forgiven.

Why perch ye here,
Where mortals to their Maker bend?
Can your pure spirits fear
The God ye never could offend?"

The words were printed precisely as they were first written. The hymn-book itself long ago mysteriously disappeared; and neither that nor the autograph copy of the lines as originally written is now known to exist. The lines exist in Mr. Sprague's handwriting, but not the copy which was first written.

Between the years 1823 and 1827 Mr. Sprague was a member of the City Council. This is the only instance in which he could be persuaded to hold public office. Here he took active part in public debate, and fulfilled most acceptably the duties of his position.

Twice Mr. Sprague accepted invitations to discourse in prose. Once, at the request of the city of Boston, he delivered the oration, July 4, 1825. This production was so popular that not less than six editions were rapidly called for. Some unscrupulous plagiarist at the West is said to have taken this oration and to have repeated it before the public as his own. The triumph gained by this borrowed plumage was of short duration. The excellence of the original was of too decided a character to allow such robbery escaping detection. The second address was on Temperance, in 1827. This was a discourse of great directness and power, and exerted a marked influence.

Aside from these productions, Mr. Sprague confined himself in his literary labors to poetry; and in this field we may be tempted to think that he appeared but too seldom. Evidently not quantity, but quality, was his aim; and in this doubtless he was right. Whatever he did was well done. It was remarked by John Quincy Adams, that Mr. Sprague's poem on Art "comprised in forty lines an encyclopædia of description." Each work from his pen was individual and masterly. Every line, every epithet, was judiciously chosen. There was a compactness of meaning, a clearness of statement, a thoroughness of finish, and a harmony of parts. Each piece was true to its own purpose, brilliant with wit, or tender with pathos; polished with artistic skill, or kindling with genius.

The following letter I received from Mr. Sprague thirty-two years ago, describing the occasion upon which the poem entitled "We are but Two" was written. The letter contains allusions to local and personal histories, which are of general interest.

Boston, Oct. 9, 1843.

Rev. R. C. Waterston.

My dear Sir, — I take pleasure in sending you the lines you asked me for. Perhaps you would like to know the story of them. You will recollect that a few years ago the city authorities extended our fine mall, so as to it entirely round the Common. By this improvement (as I suppose I must call it) some fifty or sixty tombs in the adjoining burial-ground were shut up, and their places supplied by a range of new ones, built in another part of the ground. My father's tomb was one of those disturbed. For me it had always had peculiar interest. I saw my father build it *with his own hands*, when I was a little boy, sitting on the grass and playing with the bricks round me while he was at work. A large old sycamore tree swung its branches directly over our heads.

During more than forty years I had again and again followed my dear kindred to this last resting-place (last, as I believed); and it was always my hope that in God's good time my bones might be laid there also. I wanted that the old button-wood tree's autumnal leaves should cover me. But improvement has no leisure to listen to a rhymster's sickly complaints. The tree was cut down, the mall laid out, and it became necessary to remove the tenants of our old tomb into one of the new ones. The superintending this removal fell upon my brother and myself, the surviving "two" of seven sons. Our task was performed on a cold, dreary afternoon, one of us standing at the mouth of the old tomb, while the other, as each coffin was lifted out, slowly preceded it to its new abode.

By the time we had done it was dark. We parted, each for his own home; and I could not help looking back after my companion with the saddening thought that it would not be long before that tomb must be opened again. "We *were* but two;" and of them one might soon be called to say, "I only am left."

From this little domestic incident, my dear sir, *you* will at once see that the few lines which you are pleased to compliment could hardly avoid being born, and that much, much more might have been said, had the writer drawn upon his fancy instead of his feelings.

Yours with much regard,

CHARLES SPRAGUE.

[The lines in Mr. Sprague's clear and handsome manuscript were laid before the Society. The verses have been sometimes printed with alterations made by other hands. They are here printed as he wrote them: —

THE BROTHERS.

We are but two, — the others sleep
Through death's untroubled night;
We are but two, — oh let us keep
The link that binds us bright.

Heart leaps to heart, — the sacred flood
That warms us is the same;
That good old man, — his honest blood
Alike we fondly claim.

We in one mother's arms were locked, —
 Long be her love repaid;
In the same cradle we were rocked,
 Round the same hearth we played.

Our boyish sports were all the same,
 Each little joy and woe;
Let manhood keep alive the flame,
 Lit up so long ago.

We are but two, — be that the band
 To hold us till we die;
Shoulder to shoulder let us stand,
 Till side by side we lie.

CHARLES SPRAGUE.]

The brother alluded to in these lines was George James, who died Aug. 22, 1847, four years after the foregoing letter was written. He died in the fifty-fourth year of his age. The day before his departure, twenty-eight years ago, I received the following words from Mr. Sprague: —

BOSTON, Aug. 21, 1847.

. . . . I have long ceased to use my poor pen for any other than official purposes. The last verses I ever wrote were addressed to my brother, — "We are but Two." Alas, sir, there will soon be but one! I am in much distress, for that dear brother is dying.

Yours with much esteem,

CHARLES SPRAGUE.

One cannot but feel the profoundness of his affections. With what tenacity of love he clung to those who were dear to him!

The phrase "other than official purposes" takes the mind to the scenes of Mr. Sprague's business life, and those active duties which were so constant a tax upon his time and thought. How difficult it is to associate the absorbing pursuits of business with a distinguished literary career! Yet Coleridge has some very striking remarks in his "Biographia Literaria," upon this very subject, in which he urges the course that Sprague pursued. "With no other privilege," he says, "than that of sympathy and sincere good wishes, I would address an affectionate exhortation to the youthful *literati*, grounded on my own experience. It will be but short, for the beginning, middle, and end converge to one charge: NEVER PURSUE LITERATURE AS A TRADE." "Three hours of leisure, looked forward to with delight as a change and recreation," Coleridge insists, "will abundantly suffice to realize whatever is requisite." "My dear young friend," he continues, "suppose yourself established in any honorable occupation. From the manufactory or counting-house, from the law-court or from having visited your last patient, you return at evening to your family, prepared for its social enjoyments, with the very countenances of your wife and children brightened, and their voice of welcome made doubly welcome by the knowledge that, as far as *they* are concerned, you have satisfied the demands of the day by the labor of the day. Then, when you retire into your study, in the books on your shelves you revisit so many venerable friends with whom you can converse. Your own spirit scarcely less free from personal anxieties than the great minds that in those books are still living for you!" ("Biographia Literaria," London, 1817, vol. i. p. 224.)

This view presented by Coleridge was precisely what Charles Sprague, from his own conviction, had acted upon. This imaginary picture would seem to have been taken from Mr. Sprague himself, in his domestic tranquillity and joy, in communion with the books of which he was so untiringly fond; and the statement of Coleridge appears to be verified by the literary results which Mr. Sprague, with apparent ease, accomplished.

One naturally recalls Samuel Rogers, "the banker poet," of England. But with Rogers there was no such domestic felicity. One is reminded yet more forcibly of Charles Lamb, "the gentle Elia," who must ever be associated in our thought with the South-Sea House, and the accountant's office of the East India Company, in Leadenhall Street. There, in the centre of busy interests, amid day-books and ledgers, year after year he toiled. "*Those*," Lamb would exclaim, pointing to the huge account-books which he had laboriously filled, — "*Those* are my real WORKS. There let them rest on their massy shelves, — more manuscripts in folio than ever Aquinas left!" Even so; in the brief intervals from such drudgery, which lasted over thirty years, Lamb penned his inimitable essays.

Thus also while Charles Sprague was familiarly conversant with discounts and dividends, credits and investments; intricate problems awaiting his solution, and heavy responsibilities pressing upon his mind; through all these perplexities of business, the finer sensibilities of his nature remained unscathed, and the tastes and perceptions which made him what he was received no blight. His passion for literature continued fresh, and poetic-thought welled up, a perennial fountain, — life-giving and inexhaustible.

Charles Sprague and Charles Lamb had other similarities than those connected with outward circumstance. They had both the same strong love for quaint old volumes, and were never weary of searching for the treasures they contained. "And you, my midnight darlings, my folios," Lamb would exclaim, "must I part with the intense delight of having you (huge armfuls) in my embrace? Must knowledge come to me, if it come at all, by some awkward experiment of intuition, and no longer by this familiar process of reading?" ("Elia.")

To both, the volumes they loved were an unfailing solace and delight. Mr. Sprague's house was overflowing with books, and no one knew better than he did all that was good within them. "You have come to see a happy old man," he exclaimed to me one day as I entered his room, — "a *very* happy old man, surrounded by his friends." And with a luminous smile he smote with his hand the books upon his table. "These are precious friends," he said, "and I love them more and more." Many will be reminded of his own lines to his cigar: —

"When in the lonely evening hour,
Attended but by thee,
O'er history's varied page I pore,
Man's fate in thine I see.
Oft as thy snowy column grows,
Then breaks and falls away,
I trace how mighty realms thus rose,
Thus tumbled to decay."

And we recall the lines in his Phi Beta poem: —

"'Twas heaven to lounge upon a couch, said Gray,
And read new novels through a rainy day.
Add but the Spanish weed, the bard was right;
'Tis heaven, the upper heaven of calm delight,
The world forgot, to sit at ease reclined,
While round one's head the smoky perfumes wind,
Firm in one hand the ivory folder grasped,
Scott's uncut latest by the other clasped,
'Tis heaven, the glowing, graphic page to turn,
And feel within the ruling passion burn."

Another peculiarity of Lamb's was a marked characteristic in Mr. Sprague. Both had the same partiality for the city, and loved the busy hum of streets. They had no craving for solitude, unless, like Cowper, through the loop-holes of retreat, they could peep at the world, and watch the stir of the great Babel! The moving tide of life was, to them, "better than all the waters of Damascus." London was Lamb's Paradise. The Strand and Fleet Street he affirmed he would not exchange for Skiddaw or Helvellyn. "I don't care," said Lamb, in a letter to Wordsworth, "if I never see a mountain in my life." "All these emotions," he adds, "must seem strange to you; so are your rural emotions to me." With a like taste, Mr. Sprague seldom or never went out of the city. He had no wish actually to mingle in the crowd, but he loved to look out upon it. Lamb says, "I often shed tears in the motley Strand from fulness of joy at so much life." Mr. Sprague had much of this feeling. A thousand times have I seen him at his window watching the people moving by. And as at St. Mark's, in Venice, the doves are daily fed, so it was not an unfrequent pleasure to Mr. Sprague to bestow gifts to little children as they passed by.

Meeting, one day, Mr. Sprague in the busy street, "Come with me, my dear sir," I said, "into the *country*." — "I should rejoice to do so," he replied, "but I am chained like a galley slave." — "Break your fetters," I said, "and be free." — "Ah! that," he replied with a smile, "I fear cannot be done!" Just so said Lamb. "I am a prisoner to the desk. I have been chained to that galley thirty years. I have almost grown to the wood."

Yet both Charles Sprague and Charles Lamb, though surrounded by so much that seemed antagonistic, retained their tenderness of humor, their large charity, their genial sympathies, and their nobleness of character.

Both Lamb and Sprague knew well how to

"frame matter for mirth,
Making life social, and the laggard time
To move on nimbly."

Both Charles Sprague and Charles Lamb cherished an absolute aversion to every thing that approximated to pretension and conceit. They never would profess to believe what their convictions did not accept; perhaps from that very circumstance they were at times misunderstood. That which they considered conventional had for them no special value; but they honored what they felt to be truth, and desired to plant their feet on solid foundations.

To a friend who called to visit Mr. Sprague in his last illness, he emphatically said, pointing to Christ's Sermon on the Mount, "*This* is my RELIGION." Thus did he avow that it had been his earnest desire to live in accordance with Christ's requirements, and to embody in his life the Beatitudes. What is the Sermon on the Mount but the compendium of Christianity? Never, through all his writings, did Mr. Sprague utter a word which was not in harmony with this conviction:

it was alike manifest in his daily conduct and in his intercourse with his kindred, his neighbors, and mankind. The spirit that shone through all he wrote was this, that he was habitually living, to use his own language, in the presence of One

"Before whose all-beholding eyes
Ages sweep on, and empires sink and rise!"

He declares that —

"'Twere Heaven indeed
Through fields of trackless light to soar,
On Nature's charms to feed,
And *Nature's* OWN GREAT GOD ADORE."

So, on the loss of a dear friend, he follows the ascending spirit, with the eye of faith, to

"Her eternal home,
That bright abode where sorrow ne'er can come;
There, in the likeness that her Maker drew,
Ye weeping ones, *she waits* to WELCOME YOU."

Observe how he describes, on another occasion, a friend, with prophetic vision, — beholding the splendors to come: —

"Thine eyes one moment caught A GLORIOUS LIGHT!
As if to thee, in that dread hour, 'twere given
To *know* on earth, what faith believes of Heaven!"

He then adds, —

"In my last hour be Heaven so kind to me!
I ask no more than this, — to die like thee."

Listen as he pours forth his earnest supplications to the Infinite mind: —

"On every soul
Shed the incense of thy grace,
While our anthem-echoes roll
Round the consecrated place;
While thy holy page we read,
While the prayers thou lov'st ascend,
While thy cause thy servants plead, —
Fill this house, our God and Friend.

Fill it now, — oh fill it long!
So when death shall call us home,
Still to thee, in many a throng,
May our children's children come.
Bless them, Father, long and late;
Blot their sins, their sorrows dry;
Make this place to them the gate,
LEADING TO THY COURTS ON HIGH."

Gradually the infirmities of age came upon him, his manly strength slowly giving way; but through all, to the very last, his intellectual powers continued unimpaired. Without a murmur he bore up under physical pain. Cheerfully he contemplated the final event, and became at last even anxious to go. "Say I am ready," was the message he sent, with his love, to his absent friends, and thus, peacefully as an infant sinks to its quiet slumber, on Thursday, January 21, at half-past eleven o'clock, in the eighty-fifth year of his age, he passed away.

In the same burial-place in which he describes himself as a little boy seated upon the grass watching his father with his own hands building a tomb, and to which, in after years, he had seen the dust of his parents and his kindred gathered, — in that same burial-place all that was mortal of Charles Sprague now reposes.

Most fitting it seems that there, in the midst of that busy life he loved, he should rest, — there where the young and the old in their daily walks are constantly passing. Faithful, industrious, and with an unbending integrity, he lived a spotless and childlike life. Strong in his affections, simple in his tastes, with an unchanging love for goodness and for truth, he was in himself, to those who knew and loved him, more, far more, than he ever embodied in the best he ever wrote; a broader, loftier, and more noble spirit, which language could never express. The sweetest and the grandest lines he penned were but a faint echo of that heavenly harmony which breathed through his soul.

To those who knew him, however imperfectly, his was a simple, truthful, and beautiful life; and that life has left behind quickening and inspiring memories.

Standing here by his grave, let us listen to his own words, as if his voice were still speaking to us: —

"And is this all, — this mournful doom?
Beams no glad light beyond the tomb?
Mark how yon clouds in darkness ride;
They do not quench the orb they hide;
Still there it wheels, — the tempest o'er,
In a bright sky to burn once more;
So, far above the clouds of time,
Faith can behold a world sublime, —
There, when the storms of life are past,
The light beyond shall break at last."

www.ingramcontent.com/pod-product-compliance
Lightning Source LLC
LaVergne TN
LVHW020636110826
845149LV00004B/1216

9781418190903